I0192122

FROM LOVERS' LIPS
TO THEIR FINGERTIPS

FROM LOVERS' LIPS TO THEIR FINGERTIPS

A CELEBRATION OF VALENTINE'S DAY POETRY THROUGH THE AGES

COMPILED BY
CUPID AND HIS STAFF
ASSISTED BY GERARD P. NECASTRO

THE PRIMAVERA PRESS
2017

From Lovers' Lips to Their Fingertips
A Celebration of Valentine's Day Poetry Through the Ages
Copyright © 2017 by Gerard P. NeCastro
All rights reserved.

No part of this book may be reproduced in any form or by any electronic or mechanical means including information storage and retrieval systems without permission in writing from the publisher, except by a reviewer, who may quote brief passages in a review. Please see Credits pages at the end of this book for clarification.

Published by The Primavera Press.
First paperback edition: February, 2017.
Kindle edition: February, 2017.

Requests for further permissions or information should be made to theprimaverapress@gmail.com.

Library of Congress Control Number: 2017901950.

Authors: Please see Table of Contents.

Cover Imagery: Adapted from the frontispiece of *The Book of Saint Valentine*. Boston: Small, Maynard, & Co., 1907.

Copyright © 2017 Gerard P. NeCastro, The Primavera Press
All rights reserved.

ISBN-10: 0-9894263-6-X
ISBN-13: 978-0-9894263-6-7
The Primavera Press

http://www.primaverapress.com

FOR TRUE LOVERS EVERYWHERE

TABLE OF CONTENTS

PREFACE
A JOURNEY OF THE HEART

L ove, they say, makes the world go round. That's true enough. There is perhaps nothing that motivates us more than love; nothing that absorbs us, that matters to us, and that makes us what we are, the way that love does. When we think about the power of love, we might ask, how could we fully express our love unless we had the language to do so? In effect, where would we be without the words to express our love?

In the twenty-first century we take the language of love for granted. We have industries of film, books, flowers, and gifts that thrive with the language of love, but there was a time when this language did not exist. Can you imagine such a time? Can you imagine a time when there were no love stories, no romantic dialogues, no love poems, and no valentines? Indeed, there was such a time, but the human heart has taken a long journey since then.

If we look hard enough, we can see some expressions of love in the most ancient of civilizations, but these instances are brief and rare. Likewise, if we look at the works of a handful of authors from more recent, but still ancient, times, such as Sappho or Ovid or Horace, we may find more discussion of love, but very little of it is personal or heart-felt.

In a certain way, Saint Valentine began what we recognize as sending valentines, so this had the potential for beginning a trend. Valentine, a Christian living in the Roman Empire, had converted many people to Christianity, one of whom was a magistrate whose daughter was blind. Because of Valentine's refusal to change to the state religion and perhaps because he was, against the will of Emperor Claudius II, marrying Roman soldiers to their sweethearts he was executed. On the day he was to be executed, February 14, 270, he famously sent a flower, a crocus, and a note to the magistrate's blind daughter, saying, "From Your Valentine," which, because of Valentine's miraculous powers, his prayers and her faith, and/or his medical treatments, she could now see, and read. Valentine's note, it is often observed, was not unlike notes on the slips of paper that young Roman women during the Feast of Lupercalia placed in an urn, from which young men drew their names (a sort of early dating service).

This tradition from Lupercalia largely disappeared with the end of the Roman era (around 500), and little of any love poetry seems to have been produced in the following centuries. In fact, it is not until the latter part of the Middle Ages that we can find a significant body of work that uses the language of love, a language that was largely invented at this time. Such a development may seem unusual in an era that is known for strict religious codes, conservative social controls, and general doom and gloom (though many now argue that this era was not so "dark" and not very different from our own contemporary society), but there was indeed a blossoming of the language of love at this time, particularly in the form of love poetry.

This invention or development began in one sense

with the wandering minstrel poets/singers who sang of love, represented in the following pages by Bertran de Born. It began in another sense with the group of Italian poets who wrote in what came to be known as the *dolce stil novo* (the sweet new style), represented below by Guido Cavalcanti and Dante Alighieri. Dante's *La Vita Nova* (1295) is probably the first extended narrative description of the deep feelings of love that we know.[1] And in still another sense, it began with the English poet Geoffrey Chaucer, the first writer to describe Saint Valentine's Day, which was included in his *Parliament of Fowls* (1381).

With the writers of the Middle Ages came a new sort of intensity and a true passion. With that passion and language, they changed the way that we conceived of emotions, creating perhaps the largest change in the history of humankind in the way we think about ourselves and our relationships.

This present collection of poetry begins with the troubadours, continues through the Renaissance and Enlightenment, and moves well into the twentieth century, when the language of love is fully developed and well understood by almost everyone.

The poems in this collection were selected because they were unique statements about love, because they were written with the occasion of Valentine's Day in mind, or both. A few of them might boast the credential of being the first valentine ever written. Though most of them

---

[1] *The Dove's Necklace* (1022), written by Ibn Hazm (994-1064) is an earlier extensive exploration of love, but it remains at all times on a general basis, whereas Dante's work is individual.

contain the sort of sweet sentiment that we might expect for such an occasion, some are not so. Some are more intellectual, some are spiritual, and a couple are bitter. Just as there are many sides to love and many lovers, so too there are many approaches to love in our writings. Cupid and his staff hope that you enjoy the long journey of the heart that is mapped out with these writings.

Erie, Pennsylvania, USA
December 20, 2016

A NOTE ON LANGUAGE AND VERSE

Many of the selections in this volume were, unless noted otherwise, translated or modernized by the editor, usually with the assistance of other translators and editors. Newer poems were also modernized, but to lesser degrees. Though many of the earlier selections appear as prose, they were poems in their original state. They were translated as prose in hopes of retaining the accuracy of the authors' words.

FROM LOVERS' LIPS TO THEIR FINGERTIPS

A CELEBRATION OF VALENTINE'S DAY POETRY THROUGH THE AGES

COMPILED BY

CUPID AND HIS STAFF

ASSISTED BY GERARD P. NECASTRO

THE PRIMAVERA PRESS

2017

LADY, SINCE YOU DO NOT CARE
BERTRAN DE BORN
C. 1140 – C. 1215

Lady, since you do not care for me, but
prefer to keep me far away from you
(and for no good reason), the effort to
find some other who might bring me
everlasting joy seems enormous. And if
I can not find one whom I can love as
much as the lady who is now gone from
me, I shall love no one else.

Since I will never find your match, none
so lovely as you, so noble, so joyous, so
lovely in limb, so happy, so worthy, or
so beautiful in every way, I will travel
the world to seek at least one such
feature from every beautiful woman I
meet—a sort of borrowed lady—until
the time comes when you will look upon
me again with mercy.

A LADY ASKS ME
GUIDO CAVALCANTI
1250 – 1300

A lady asks me, and I must reply with
reason. It may seem bold, daring, and
even arrogant, but maybe it is inspired
from above. It is called Love, Amore, and
any who deny Love must now face the
truth! I speak to you now with knowledge,
with no expectation that the base-hearted
can understand, even with my explanation.

And I do not have the talent to prove how
Love is created or where it lives, what
power it might have or what virtues, its
essence or its movements. Nor can I show
all the delight in what we say it is "to
love."

*In this beautifully crafted poem, Cavalcanti goes on to explain
the way that love comes about, how it enters the mind, chases
reason from the mind, and takes over the will of the individual.
Through self-control, though, the individual can remain rational
while still enjoying love.*

MY LADY LOOKS SO GENTLE
DANTE ALIGHIERI
1265 – 1321

My lady looks so gentle and so pure
    When yielding salutation by the way,
    That the tongue trembles and has nought[2] to say,
And the eyes, which fain would see, may not endure.
And still, amid the praise she hears secure,
    She walks with humbleness for her array;
    Seeming a creature sent from Heaven to stay
On earth, and show a miracle made sure.
    She is so pleasant in the eyes of men
    That through the sight the inmost heart doth gain
A sweetness which needs proof to know it by:
    And from between her lips there seems to move
    A soothing essence that is full of love,
Saying for ever to the spirit, "Sigh!"

Translated by Dante Gabriel Rossetti (1828 – 1882).

---

[2] Nought. Nothing.

WHERE THE HEART IS
JOHN GOWER
1330 – 1408

Saint Valentine governs the love and nature of all the
birds, and for this reason each bird selects from its
kind, true, and honest companion, as it so inclines.
They all agree to do so together, and in this way one
bird alone gladly leaves all the others, because
Nature teaches that where the heart is, the body must
follow.

My sweet lady, I assure you that in the same way I
have chosen you. Above all the others you are on
high, so supremely sacred to my love that nothing is
missing. And so I wish to serve you joyfully with
heart and body, because by reason it is proven,
where the heart is, the body must follow.

Furthermore, always keep in mind the fate of
Alcyone and Ceyx, and how God transformed their
bodies into birds. My wishes would be entirely the
same, so that without envy and trouble from people
we would be able at leisure to fly together fully free
for our worries. Where the heart is, the body must
follow.

My beautiful bird, toward whom my thoughts shall
always fly, without any doubts, take this writing,
because I know in truth, where the heart is, the body
must follow.

WHOSOEVER REMAINS ALONE
JOHN GOWER
1330 – 1408

Saint Valentine, greater than any emperor, holds a parliament and assembly of all the birds, who come on his day, where the female takes her mate in perfect love. But for my own part, I am unable to make any such comparison, for whosoever remains alone is unable to have great joy.

As the Phoenix is alone in its home in the region of Arabia, so too my lady remains alone in the place of her love, where, if I wish it or not, she cares not about my pleas, because I do not know how to find the pathway of love. Whosoever remains alone is unable to have great joy.

Oh, how Nature is full of favor to those birds who have their choice of lovers! Oh, if, instead of my state, I might be in their very situation! Nature is more able than reason, and in my state it senses very well the path. Whosoever remains alone is unable to have great joy.

Each gentle lady tercelet has her falcon, but I am missing what I desire. My lady, this is the end of my song. Whosoever remains alone is unable to have great joy.

The Parliament of Fowls (A Selection)
Geoffrey Chaucer
1340 – 1400

As noted above, Chaucer's poem contains the first mention of Saint Valentine's Day as a celebration of romantic love.

When I had returned to the sweet and green garden
that I spoke of, I walked forth to comfort myself.
Then I noticed how there sat a queen who
surpassed in beauty every other creature, just as
the brilliant summer sun passes the stars in
brightness. This noble goddess Nature was set
upon a flowery hill in a verdant glade. All her
halls and bowers were wrought of branches
according to the art and moderation of Nature.

And there was not any bird that is made through
pro-creation that was not ready in her presence to
hear her and receive her judgment. For this was
Saint Valentine's Day, when every bird of every
kind that people can imagine comes to this place
to choose its mate.

♥

And when this work was all brought to an end,
Nature gave every bird his mate by just accord,
and they went their way. Ah, Lord! The bliss and
joy that they made! For each of them took the
other in his wings, and wound their necks about
each other, ever thanking the noble goddess of
Nature. But first were chosen birds to sing, as was

always their custom year by year to sing a song at
their departure, to honor Nature and give her
pleasure. The tune, I believe, was made in France.
The words were such as you may here find in
these verses, as I remember them.

Who loves well forgets slowly

"Welcome, summer, with sunshine soft,
The winter's tempest you will break,
And drive away the long nights black!

"Saint Valentine, throned aloft,
Thus little birds sing for your sake:
Welcome, summer, with sunshine soft,
The winter's tempest you will shake!

"Good cause have they to glad them oft,
His own true-love each bird will take;
Blithe may they sing when they awake,
Welcome, summer, with sunshine soft,
The winter's tempest you will break,
And drive away the long nights black!"

And with the shouting that the birds raised, as they
flew away when their song was done, I awoke

*These two selections are from the middle of the poem, when the
narrator, in the middle of a dream, comes upon Nature and the
many birds who have come to choose their mates, especially a
royal female eagle. Although she is unable to decide, the poem
still ends happily (in the second passage) with the birds
rejoicing for the gift of love. The poem had dozens of imitations
over the next hundred years.*

LEGEND OF GOOD WOMEN (A SELECTION)
GEOFFREY CHAUCER
1340 – 1400

On the branches some sang sweet songs of love and
spring, in honor and praise of their mates, and for the new,
joyous summer; it was a joy to listen. Upon those branches
full of soft blossoms, in their delight the birds often moved
about and sang,

> "Blessed be Saint Valentine!
> For on his day I chose you to be mine,
> My sweetheart, and never have I repented."

And then they joined their beaks, and they paid honor and
tenderness to each other, and then performed other
ceremonies pleasing to love and nature. (I listened carefully
to their song, for I dreamed I understood their meaning.)

THE COMPLAINT OF MARS (A SELECTION)
GEOFFREY CHAUCER
1340 – 1400

Rejoice, you birds, at the gray dawn; lo, Venus, arisen among yonder ruddy streaks! And you fresh flowers, honor this day, for you will open when the sun rises. But you lovers that are in fear, flee, lest wicked tongues discover you. Behold the sun yonder, the candle of Jealousy!

Stained with tears and with wounded heart, take your leave; and, with Saint John as your guarantee, take comfort somewhat in your bitter sorrows; the time will come again when your woes shall cease. A heavy morning is not too great a price for a joyous night. Thus, Saint Valentine, I heard a bird sing upon your day, before the sun rose.

And yet sang this bird: "Waken all, I counsel you. And you who have not humbly chosen your mates in good time, make your faithful choice now. And you who have chosen as I prescribe, renew your homage at least; confirm it, to last perpetually, and patiently accept what befalls you."

THE COMPLAINT OF LOVE (A SELECTION)
GEOFFREY CHAUCER
1340 – 1400

I have ever been, and ever shall be,
however I journey on, either to life or to
death, your humble, true man. You are
to me my beginning and end, the sun
which illumines the bright and shining
star.[3] By God and my word, it is my
intent always and anew to love you
freshly. Live or die, I will never repent
of it!

I write this complaint, this woeful song
and lament, on Saint Valentine's Day,
when every bird shall choose his mate,
to her whose I am wholly and ever shall
be, her who has never yet given me her
mercy. And yet I will serve her
evermore and love her best, though she
may let me perish.

---

[3] Star. Probably Venus, since the next line mentions love.

THE BOOK OF CUPID, OR
THE CUCKOO AND THE NIGHTINGALE (A SELECTION)
JOHN CLANVOWE
1341 – 1391

In May I had slept very little, and it was not
pleasing to me that any heart that Love
would strike with his fiery arrow should be
sleepy. But as I lay the other night wide
awake, I thought about how lovers believed
that it was a sign (and among them it was a
common saying) that it would be good to
hear the nightingale (rather than the silly
cuckoo) sing.

And then I thought, as soon as it was day, I
would go somewhere to see if I might hear a
nightingale; for I had not yet heard one all
this year, and it was at that point the third
night of May.

And then, as soon as I could perceive the
light of day, I would no longer wait in my
bed, but I went alone into the nearby woods,
boldly, and made my way down by a brook-
side until I came to a land of white and
green. I had never been in one so beautiful;
the ground was green, sprinkled with
daisies. The flowers and the grass were both
high, all green and white, as far as the eye
could see.

I sat down there among the pretty flowers
and saw the birds dance out of her homes
where they had been resting all night. They
were so joyful for the day's light that they
began in May to sing their regular services!

They knew that service entirely by heart.
There were many lovely unusual notes.
Some sang loud, as if they were
complaining, some sang softly, and some
sang all out, with full throat.

They preened themselves and made
themselves joyful. They danced and leapt on
the branches, and everywhere I looked there
were two and two together. This is the way
they chose one another each year in
February on Saint Valentine's Day.

And the river that I sat next to it made such
a noise as it was running. It seemed to me
that it mixed with the harmony of the birds.
It was the best melody that anyone could
ever hear.

And because of the delight I gained from
that music, I fell, I don't know how, into
such a swoon and slumber, not completely
asleep nor fully awake; and in that swoon it
seemed like I heard singing that sorry bird,
the ignorant Cuckoo. It was on a nearby tree,
and who got the worst of it but me? "By

God," I said, "who died upon the cross, have pity on me, and on your awful voice! I have little joy now from your cry."

And as I chided this Cuckoo, I heard in the next bush a Nightingale sing so lustily that her clear voice rang throughout the entire huge green woods.

"Ah, good Nightingale!" I said then. "You have been gone a little too long from here; for the stupid Cuckoo has been singing songs instead of you; I pray to God that he will burn in the fires of Hell!"

But now I'd like to tell you an amazing thing. As I lay there for a long time in that swoon, It seems, I could understand what the birds said, what they meant, and what their intention was. In short, I had a good idea what they were saying.

And then heard the Nightingale say, "Now, good Cuckoo, go somewhere away, and let us that can sing remain here; for every creature hates to hear you, your songs are so tedious, by God!"

This debate between the two birds continues at length, the Nightingale in favor of love and the Cuckoo against, until love, of course, wins.

SAINT VALENTINE'S DREAM (A SELECTION)
OTTON DE GRANSON
1346 – 1397

It is very comforting to think, if only to
pass the time of day once in a while. It
sets the body at rest, in great repose and
at great peace, which calms the heart.

Day and night, a man may consider
what pleases him or what harms him.
And so it is that nobody will ever be
able to detect If his thoughts are foolish
or wise until he himself makes them
known by speech or by action. And yet
it gives great relief to the heart when a
man is depressed or tired and so wishes
to rest.

He can think about such things until he
falls asleep, and while sleeping, he will
dream some marvelous thing, pleasant
or troubling for him, just as I did on the
morning of the feast of Saint Valentine.
That night I laid awake, as my heart had
troubled me with various thoughts
which haven't entirely gone away.

I fell asleep on a bed where I was lying,
and as I slept it seemed to me that on the
previous day I had left behind a ruby

ring and a diamond one in a garden, and
I had to go that morning to search for
them. But when I came near to the
garden where I thought I would find my
rings, I saw there many birds, white and
black; tame and wild; fledgling, molting,
and nestling; from the trees, the woods,
the fields, and the rivers; from houses
and from dovecotes. Small and large,
they were all there, and from the sea
many types of birds came.

This poem is similar to Chaucer's Parliament of Fowls, *except
that it reaches a tidy conclusion to the eagle's choice of a mate.
It should be noted that Granson wrote a total of nine Valentine's
Day poems.*

GOOD THOMAS THE FRIAR
ANONYMOUS
LATE 1300S?

Though it may be all in vain,
I wish God's blessing and mine,
To you, good Thomas the Friar,
My own gentle Valentine

Thow it be alle other wyn
Godys blessing have he and myn,
My none gentle Volontyn,
Good Tomas the frere.

This is perhaps the first valentine. It is from a fourteenth-century manuscript called Harley MS 2241.

SONG OF THE ROSE
CHRISTINE DE PISAN
1364 – 1431

The sight of it, the thought that I was
charged with it,[4] delighted me. I hardly
think that I am at all worthy, and yet I
am eager that none will fail. Since the
charge is given to me to take action, I
must not neglect to do my duty. If I do, I
will not be blamed for doing careless
work. So I have written this tale, entered
all the details, and given the general
design of it, just how it happened and
where it took place, so everyone can
know of it.

May everyone, old and young, decide to
enlist in the Order of the Rose; but may
nobody enlist who will not fulfill their
vows, for they would cause immense
harm.

Ladies, therefore, who are in love and
hope for the best things, I wish for you
pure love, with no evil villainy, or
malice. Believe it or not, in true love
there is nothing but good. For those

---

[4] She has been charged with the administration of the Order of the Rose,
all members of which must vow to defend the honor of women.

women everywhere who cherish their
honor above all, whose hearts are noble,
whether here or elsewhere, I bestow to
you, in service to the goddess Venus,
complete authority to give the lovely
Order of the Rose out to noble people,
and to do so in places where they think
it will be well-used by those who are
sincerely lacking in it. But if someone
should take the vow and stray from his
word at a later time, may that soul b
disgraced, despised by men and women
alike, as the goddess Venus wishes, who
has given us our instructions.

Thus I will end, as the time has come. I
ask God to grant a good life and
Paradise to those who will read my
poem, which was composed this Day,
Saint Valentine's Day, when lovers
select in early morning their sweethearts
for the year, since that's the law of this
day.

A STRING OF BEADS
CHRISTINE DE PISAN
1364 – 1431

Dear Friend,

I have chosen you today, for it is the custom
on the first day of Spring to take a friend for
the year, and to show one's love by
exchanging green stings of beads. I have
chosen you, and you will have my love. You
have suffered, but you will be rewarded.

Now, so that I may keep the custom on Saint
Valentine's Day, take my string of beads,
and give me yours. I will love you, no
matter what happens.

Depending on the actual date of the "Good Thomas the Friar"
poem (included above), "A String of Beads," written in 1401, might
also be the first valentine.

TO MY SOVEREIGN LADY
JOHN LYDGATE
1370 – 1451

I have no suitable or worthy English with which to
honor you, lady, the joy of my heart, as clean as
ivory; therefore I will resign myself into your hand,
until the time comes when you wish to give me aid,
to help my making both flourish and flower in your
name. Then will I show how I burn in love, making
songs to praise your name.

For if I could sing of love before your excellence, I
would gladly sing what I feel, and forever stand,
lady, in thy presence, to show openly how I love you
joyfully. And though your heart may be made of
steel, to you I would sing without any lie, "I have all
my trust in you."

With a burning heart my breast has burst into
flames; the ardent hope that pricks my heart is dead,
and the hope to gain the love of her whom I desire is
gone. I mean you, sweet one, most pleasant and
courteous. And I know well that it is not the fault of
me, who sings for you, as I may, mourning for your
departure. Alone I live, alone.

Though I might attempt such a thing, I wish to make
no other choice. Look up, all you lovers, and be
joyful as you await Saint Valentine's Day, for I have
chosen one whom I may never forsake!

A Valentine to Her Who Excels Them All
John Lydgate
1370 – 1451

Saint Valentine, of custom year by year,
Men have an practice in this region
To look and search Cupid's Calendar,
And choose their choice, by great affection;
Such as are pricked with Cupid's emotion,
Taking their choice as their chance my fall:
But I love one who excels them all.

Some choose for fairness and for great beauty,
Some for estate, and some so for richness,
Some for nobility, some bounty,
Some for their poverty and gentleness,
Some for their pleasantness, some for their goodness,
Just as the chance of their sort might fall,
But I love one who excels them all.

I chose that flower, long gone since your,
And every year my choice shall renew,
Upon this day confirm it evermore,
She is in cove so steadfast and so true;
Who loves her best, shall the day never rue,
If such a grace unto his sort may fall,
Whom I have chosen, for she excels them all.

Lydgate continues by naming dozens of famous and virtuous women in seventy lines and then focuses on Mary, the mother of Jesus Christ.

And if I shall her name specify,
That all may know who she shall be,
This good and fresh one's called Mary,
A branch of kings, that sprang out of Jesse,
That made the Lord through her humility
To let his gold dew into her breast down fall,
To bear the fruit which should save us all.

*After a lengthy description of Mary, Lydgate concludes the poem
and then in the Envoy (or dedication), he sends his poem to
Katherine, the French wife of Henry V of England.*

To follow their hearts everyone is free,
(To even say no), in love will they choose;
In choice of love there is great liberty
Every season, whether it will thaw or freeze;
And for my part, because I wish not choose,
Into my choice there may no trouble fall,
I have chosen one who excels them all.

From year to year, for negligence or pain,
Beyond all change and all newfangled-ness,
Saint Valentine I shall not disdain
On your own day, in token of steadfastness,
Rather I shall confirm in secure-ness
My choice for now, so as it may befall,
To love her best, who excels them all.

Envoy

Noble princess, branch of fleur-de-lis,
Whose goodness though the world does shine,
So well advised, so prudent, and so wise,

Saint Louis' blood, and of that noble line!
Lowly beseech I, confirm and determine
To give me love, so as it may befall,
To love her best who excels them all.

With humble heart beseeching that virgin,
Who is most fair, most bounteous and good,
To Henry Sixth, his Mother Katherine,
To shed her grace, and to their noble blood;
And Christ Jesus, who died upon the Rood,[5]
Have on us mercy, when we for help call,
For love of her who excels them all.

---

[5] Rood. Cross, or crucifix.

Charter of the Court of Love (A Selection)
Alain Chartier
1385 – 1446

There will be a solemn and joyous Feast of the Court of Love on the first Sunday of each month, beginning in the month of February. Moreover, on the day of my Lord Saint Valentine, on the fourteenth day of February, when the little birds begin again their sweet song when they perceive the return of the new Spring season, there at the church of Saint Catherine du Val des Ecoliers in Paris will be sung a mass to honor this blessed martyr on the same day that this charter will be given a public reading.

And on each year on Saint Valentine's Day a dinner will and a joyous celebration will be held for the entire court. If Saint Valentine's Day should fall on a Friday or on a fasting day or on a church vigil, the feast will be transferred to the following Sunday. On this feast day, each of the subjects of Saint Valentine is to compose a ballad of love on a theme of his own choice, and appointed ladies will award prizes to the best of the poets.

There will also be a special feast each year in May (the date to be named by the prince), and still another similar festivity will be observed on one of the five feast days of the Blessed Virgin Mary, who is the advocate of all true loving hearts.

FAREWELL TO LOVE
CHARLES OF ORLEANS
1394 – 1465

I am already sick of love,
My very gentle Valentine,
Since you were born too soon for me,
And I was born too late for you.
God forgives the one who has estranged
Me from you for this whole year.
I am already sick of love,
My very gentle Valentine.

Well might I have suspected
That such a destiny would have,
Thus come to pass this day.
How much that Love would have commanded!
I am already sick of love,
My very gentle Valentine.

This poem, written in 1415, is often referred to as the first valentine, though other pieces in this collection might have preceded it. Original translation by Isobel Costa; adapted by Cupid and his staff.

PHILLIS INAMORATA
LANCELOT ANDREWS
1555 – 1626

Come, be my valentine!
I'll gather eglantine,
Cowslips and sops-in-wine,
    With fragrant roses.
Down by thy Phillis sit,
She will white lilies get,
And daffodilies fit
    To make thee posies.

I have a milk-white lamb,
New-taken from the dam,
It comes where'er I am
    When I call "Willy:"
I have a wanton kid
Under my apron hid,
A colt that ne'er was rid,
    A pretty filly.

I bear in sign of love
A sparrow in my glove,
And in my breast a dove,
    This shall be all thine:
Besides of sheep a flock,
Which yieldeth many a lock,
And this shall be thy stock:
    Come, be my valentine!

For His Valentine
William Fowler
1560 – 1612

Prepare and send, as papists do,
O poets, your finest rhyme,
And celebrate the memory
Of blessed Saint Valentine.

Sound forth your voice, and sing his praise
With learned verses fine,
And with my ladies resound the glory
Of blessed Saint Valentine.

Of all the saints within the heaven,
Both goodly and divine,
None more I love or honor more
Than blessed Saint Valentine.

For he by lot to me her name[6]
Bestowed, as if a sign,
And promised love and constancy,
The blessed Saint Valentine.

Take in good part their hasty lines,
O you sweet mistress mine,
And, if you please, a ring or charm
Send to your valentine.

---

[6] By lot. There was a practice in Europe, which dates back to ancient Rome (particularly the Feast of Lupercalia), where the names of young women were placed in a large urn, from which the young women drew their names. Thus they were to spend the day together.

But if you fail, I swear I shall,
Suppose my heart repine,
Burn in the fire your gracious name,
And curse Saint Valentine.

TO HIS VALENTINE
MICHAEL DRAYTON
1563 – 1631

Muse, bid the Morn awake!
    Sad Winter now declines,
Each bird doth choose a mate,
    This day's Saint Valentine's.
For that good bishop's sake
Get up and let us see
What beauty it shall be
    That Fortune us assigns.

But lo, in happy hour,
    The place wherein she lies,
In yonder climbing tower,
    Gilt by the glittering rise;
O Jove! that in a shower,
As once that thunderer did,
When he in drops lay hid,
    That I could her surprise.

Her canopy I'll draw,
    With spangled plumes bedight,
No mortal ever saw
    So ravishing a sight;
That it the gods might awe,
And powerfully transpierce
The globy universe,
    Out-shooting every light.

My lips I'll softly lay
    Upon her heavenly cheek,
Dyed like the dawning day,
    As polished ivory sleek;
And in her ear I'll say,
"O thou bright morning-star,
'Tis I that come so far,
    My valentine to seek.

"Each little bird, this tide,
    Doth choose her loved peer,
Which constantly abide
    In wedlock all the year,
As nature is their guide:
So may we two be true,
This year, nor change for new,
    As turtles coupled were. —

"Let's laugh at them that choose
    Their valentines by lot.
To wear their names that use,
    Whom idly they have got;
Such poor choice we refuse,
Saint Valentine befriend;
We thus this morn may spend,
    Else, Muse, awake her not."

LET ME NOT TO THE MARRIAGE OF TRUE MINDS
WILLIAM SHAKESPEARE
1564 - 1616

Let me not to the marriage of true minds
Admit impediments. Love is not love
Which alters when it alteration finds,
Or bends with the remover to remove.
O no! it is an ever-fixed mark
That looks on tempests and is never shaken;
It is the star to every wandering bark,
Whose worth's unknown, although his height be taken.
Love's not Time's fool, though rosy lips and cheeks
Within his bending sickle's compass come;
Love alters not with his brief hours and weeks,
But bears it out even to the edge of doom.
If this be error and upon me proved,
I never writ, nor no man ever loved.

Though this poem and the next are not strictly speaking
Valentine's Day poems, they are two of the finest articulations of
love ever written.

MY MISTRESS' EYES ARE NOTHING LIKE THE SUN
WILLIAM SHAKESPEARE
1564 - 1616

My mistress' eyes are nothing like the sun;
Coral is far more red than her lips' red;
If snow be white, why then her breasts are dun;[7]
If hairs be wires,[8] black wires grow on her head.
I have seen roses damasked, red and white,
But no such roses see I in her cheeks;
And in some perfumes is there more delight
Than in the breath that from my mistress reeks.[9]
I love to hear her speak, yet well I know
That music hath a far more pleasing sound;
I grant I never saw a goddess go;
My mistress, when she walks, treads on the ground.
    And yet, by heaven, I think my love as rare
    As any she belied with false compare.

---

[7] Dun. Brownish.
[8] Wires. Filaments.
[9] Reeks. Emits.

OPHELIA'S SONG
WILLIAM SHAKESPEARE
1564 – 1616

To-morrow is Saint Valentine's day,
All in the morning betime,[10]
And I a maid at your window,
To be your Valentine.
Then up he rose, and donned his clothes,
And dupped[11] the chamber-door;
Let in the maid, that out a maid
Never departed more.
By Gis[12] and by Saint Charity,
Alack, and fie for shame!
Young men will do't, if they come to't;
By cock,[13] they are to blame.
Quoth she, before you tumbled me,
You promised me to wed.
So would I ha' done, by yonder sun,
An[14] thou hadst not come to my bed.

Hamlet, Act 4, Scene 5

---

[10] Betime. Early.
[11] Dupped. Opened. (Do up.)
[12] By Gis. By Jesus.
[13] By cock. By God.
[14] An. If.

33

AN EPITHALAMION, OR MARRIAGE SONG ON THE
LADY ELIZABETH AND COUNT PALATINE BEING
MARRIED ON SAINT VALENTINE'S DAY
JOHN DONNE
1573 – 1631

I

Hail Bishop Valentine, whose day this is;
    All the air is thy diocese,
    And all the chirping choristers
And other birds are thy parishioners;
    Thou marriest every year
The lyric lark, and the grave whispering dove,
The sparrow that neglects his life for love,
The household bird with the red stomacher;
    Thou makest the blackbird speed as soon,
As doth the goldfinch, or the halcyon;
The husband cock looks out, and straight is sped,
And meets his wife, which brings her feather-bed.
This day more cheerfully than ever shine;
This day, which might enflame thyself, old Valentine.

II

Till now, thou warmd'st with multiplying loves
    Two larks, two sparrows, or two doves;
    All that is nothing unto this;
For thou this day couplest two phoenixes;
    Thou makst a taper see
What the sun never saw, and what the ark
—Which was of fouls and beasts the cage and park—
Did not contain, one bed contains, through thee;

34

Two phoenixes, whose joined breasts
Are unto one another mutual nests,
Where motion kindles such fires as shall give
Young phoenixes, and yet the old shall live;
Whose love and courage never shall decline,
But make the whole year through, thy day, O Valentine.

III

Up then, fair phoenix bride, frustrate the sun;
    Thyself from thine affection
    Takest warmth enough, and from thine eye
All lesser birds will take their jollity.
    Up, up, fair bride, and call
Thy stars from out their several boxes, take
Thy rubies, pearls, and diamonds forth, and make
Thyself a constellation of them all;
    And by their blazing signify
That a great princess falls, but doth not die.
Be thou a new star, that to us portends
Ends of much wonder; and be thou those ends.
Since thou dost this day in new glory shine,
May all men date records from this day, Valentine.

IV

Come forth, come forth, and as one glorious flame
    Meeting another grows the same,
    So meet thy Frederick, and so
To an inseparable union go,
    Since separation
Falls not on such things as are infinite,
Nor things, which are but one, can disunite.
You're twice inseparable, great, and one;

Go then to where the bishop stays,
To make you one, his way, which divers ways
Must be effected; and when all is past,
And that you're one, by hearts and hands made fast,
You two have one way left, yourselves to entwine,
Besides this bishop's knot, of Bishop Valentine.

V
But O, what ails the sun, that here he stays,
     Longer to-day than other days?
     Stays he new light from these to get?
And finding here such stars, is loth to set?
     And why do you two walk,
So slowly paced in this procession?
Is all your care but to be look'd upon,
And be to others spectacle, and talk?
     The feast with gluttonous delays
Is eaten, and too long their meat they praise;
The masquers come late, and I think, will stay,
Like fairies, till the cock crow them away.
Alas! did not antiquity assign
A night as well as day, to thee, old Valentine?

VI
They did, and night is come; and yet we see
     Formalities retarding thee.
     What mean these ladies, which—as though
They were to take a clock in pieces—go
     So nicely about the bride?
A bride, before a "Good-night" could be said,
Should vanish from her clothes into her bed,
As souls from bodies steal, and are not spied.

But now she's laid; what though she be?
Yet there are more delays, for where is he?
He comes and passeth through sphere after sphere;
First her sheets, then her arms, then anywhere.
Let not this day, then, but this night be thine;
Thy day was but the eve to this, O Valentine.

VII

Here lies a she sun, and a he moon there;
　　　She gives the best light to his sphere;
　　　Or each is both, and all, and so
They unto one another nothing owe;
　　　And yet they do, but are
So just and rich in that coin which they pay,
That neither would, nor needs forbear, nor stay;
Neither desires to be spared nor to spare.
　　　They quickly pay their debt, and then
Take no acquittances, but pay again;
They pay, they give, they lend, and so let fall
No such occasion to be liberal.
More truth, more courage in these two do shine,
Than all thy turtles have and sparrows, Valentine.

VIII

And by this act these two phoenixes
　　　Nature again restorèd is;
　　　For since these two are two no more,
There's but one phoenix still, as was before.
　　　Rest now at last, and we—
As satyrs watch the sun's uprise—will stay
Waiting when your eyes opened let out day,
Only desired because your face we see.

Others near you shall whispering speak,
And wagers lay, at which side day will break,
And win by observing, then, whose hand it is
That opens first a curtain, hers or his:
This will be tried to-morrow after nine,
Till which hour, we thy day enlarge, O Valentine.

AN ELIZABETHAN VALENTINE
ANONYMOUS
FROM AN ALBUM DATED 1583

When Slumber first unclouds my brain,
    And thought is free
And Sense refreshed renews her reign, —
    I think of Thee

When next in prayer to God above
    I bend my knee,
Then when I pray for those I love, —
    I pray for Thee.

And when the duties of the day
    Demand of me
To rise and journey on life's way, —
    I work for Thee.

Or if perchance I sing some lay,
    Whate'er it bee;
All that the idle verses say, —
    They say of Thee.

For if an eye whose liquid light
    Gleams like the sea,
They sing, or tresses brown and bright, —
    They sing of Thee.

And if a weary mood, or sad,
    Possesses me,
One thought can all times make me glad,

The thought of Thee.

And when once more upon my bed,
    Full wearily,
In sweet repose I lay my head, —
    I dream of Thee.

In short, one only wish I have —
    To live for Thee;
Or gladly if one pang 'twould save
    I'd die for Thee.

LOVE UPBRAIDING
(TO BE HIS VALENTINE)
ROBERT HERRICK
1591 – 1674

Choose me your valentine;
    Next let us marry;
Love to the death will pine,
    If we long tarry.

Promise and keep your vows,
    Or vow ye never;
Love's doctrine disawows
    Troth-breakers ever.

You have broke promise twice,
    Dear, to undo me;
If you prove faithless thrice,
    None then will woo thee.

TO HIS VALENTINE, ON SAINT VALENTINE'S DAY
ROBERT HERRICK
1591 – 1674

Oft have I heard both Youths and Virgins say,
Birds choose their Mates, and couple too, this day:
But by their flight I never can divine,
When I shall couple with my Valentine.

SAINT VALENTINE'S DAY
HENRY KING
1592 – 1669

Now that each feathered chorister doth sing
The glad approaches of the welcome Spring:
Now Phoebus[15] darts forth his more early beam
And dips it later in the curled stream,
I should to custom prove a retrograde
Did I still dote upon my sullen shade.

Oft have the seasons finished and begun;
Days into months, those into years have run,
Since my cross stars and inauspicious fate
Doomed me to linger here without my mate
Whose loss ere since befrosting my desire,
Left me an Altar without gift or fire.

I therefore could have wished for your own sake
That Fortune had designed a nobler stake
For you to draw, than one whose fading day
Like to a dedicated taper lay
Within a tomb, and long burnt out in vain,
Since nothing there saw better by the flame.

Yet since you like your chance, I must not try
To mar it through my incapacity.
I here make title to it, and proclaim
How much you honour me to wear my name;
Who can no form of gratitude devise,

---

[15] Phoebus. Apollo, god of the sun, among other things.

But offer up myself your sacrifice.

Hail, then, my worthy lot! and may each morn
Successive springs of joy to you be born:
May your content ne'er wane until my heart
Grown bankrupt, wants good wishes to impart.
Henceforth I need not make the dust my shrine,
Nor search the grave for my lost Valentine.

THE MISTAKE
THOMAS CAREW
1595 – 1640

When on fair Celia I did spy
    A wounded heart of stone,
The wound had almost made me cry,
    Sure this heart was my own!

But when I saw it was enthroned
    In her celestial breast,
O then I it no longer owned,
    For mine was ne'er so blest.

Yet, if in highest heavens do shine,
    Each constant martyr's heart,
Then she may well give rest to mine,
    That for her sake doth smart;

Where, seated in so high a bliss,
    Though wounded, it shall live;
Death enters not in Paradise,
    The place free life doth give.

Or if the place less sacred were,
    Did but her saving eye
Bathe my sick heart in one kind tear,
    Then should I never die.

Slight balms may heal a slighter sore,
    No medicine less divine
Can ever hope for to restore
    A wounded heart like mine.

45

I'LL LOVE THEE TILL I DIE
ANONYMOUS
AROUND 1607

O Dearling Lady, sweet and kind,
Was never face so pleased my mind;
I did but see thee passing by,
And Lo! I'll love thee till I die.

TO CUPID
WILLIAM CARTWRIGHT
1611 – 1643

Thou, who didst never see the light
Nor know'st the pleasure of the sight,
But always blinded, canst not say
Now it is night, or now 'tis day:
So captivate her sense, so blind her eye,
That still she love me, yet she ne'r know why.

Thou who dost wound us with such art
We see no blood drop from the heart,
And subtly cruel leav'st no sign
To tell the blow or hand was thine,
O gently, gently wound my fair, that she
May thence believe the wound did come from thee!

I DARE NOT ASK A KISS
ANONYMOUS
AROUND 1618

I dare not ask a kiss,
I dare not beg a smile,
Lest Having that, or this,
    I might grow proud the while.

No, no, the utmost share
Of my desire shall be
Only to kiss that air
    That lately kissed thee.

TO A LADY, WITH A PAIR OF GLOVES,
ON SAINT VALENTINE'S DAY
GEORGE VILLIERS, DUKE OF BUCKINGHAM
1628 – 1687

Brimful of anger, not of love,
The champion sends his foe one glove;
But I, who have a double share
Of softer passion, send a pair.
Nor think it, dearest Celia, cruel
That I invite you to a duel;
Ready to meet you face to face,
At any time, in any place:
Nor will I leave you in the lurch,
Though you should dare to name the church;
There come equipped with all your charms,
The ring and license are my arms;
With these I mean your power to try,
And meet my charmer though I die.

GIVE ME YOUR HEART
ANONYMOUS
AROUND 1660

High state and honors to others impart,
    But give me your heart!
That treasure, that treasure alone,
    I beg for my own.
So gentle a love, so fervent a fire,
    My soul does inspire:
That treasure, that treasure alone,
    I beg for my own,
    Girt me in possessing
    So matchless a blessing!
That empire is all I would have.

YOUNG MEN AND MAIDS
ANONYMOUS (POOR ROBIN'S ALMANAC)
1670

Young men and maids, where love combines,
Each other draw for Valentines;
They clip[16] and kiss, and dance and sing,
And love like unto anything:
For young men they like to be doing,
And freely spend their coin in wooing.

---

[16] Clip. Embrace.

THE VALENTINE
ANONYMOUS, FROM WESTMINSTER DROLLERY
1672

As youthful day put on his best
    Attire to usher morn,
And she to greet her glorious guest
    Did her fair self adorn,
Up did I rise, and hide mine eyes
    As I went through the street,
Lest I should one that I despise
    Before a fairer meet.
        And why
        Was I,
    Think you, so nice and fine?
        Well did I wot
        (Who wots it not?)
    It was Saint Valentine.

In fields by Phoebus great with young
    Of flowers and hopeful buds,
Resembling thoughts that freshly sprung
    In lovers' lively bloods,
A damsel fair and fine I saw,
    So fair and finely dight,[17]
As put my heart almost in awe
    To attempt a mate so bright:
        But O
        Why so?

---

[17] Dight. Dressed.

Her purpose was like mine,
    And readily
    She said as I
"Good morrow, Valentine."

A fair of love we kept a while:
    She for each word I said
Gave me two smiles, and for each smile
    I her two kisses paid.
The violet made haste to appear,
    To be her bosom-guest,
With first primrose that grew this year,
    I purchased for l her breast:
        To me
        Gave she
    Her golden lock for mine;
        My ring of jet,
        For her bracelet,
    I gave my Valentine.

Subscribed with a line of love,
    My name for her I wrote;
In silk for me her name she wove
    Whereto this was her mot,
"As shall this year thy truth appear,
    I still, my dear, am thine;"
"Your mate today, and love for aye,
    If you so say," was mine.
        While thus
        On us
    Each other's favours shine,
        "No more have we

To change," quoth she,
"Now farewell, Valentine."

"Alas," said I, "let friends not seem
    Between themselves so strange;
The jewels both we dear'st esteem
    You know are yet to change."
She answers, "No," yet smiles as though
    Her tongue her thought denies!
Who truth of maiden's mind will know
    Must seek it in her eyes.
        She blushed,
        I wished
    Her heart as free as mine,
        She sighed and sware
        "In sooth you are
    Too wanton, Valentine."

Yet I such further favour won
    By suit and pleasing play,
She vowed what now was left undone
    Should finished be in May;
And though perplexed with such delay
    As more augments desire,
'Twixt present grief and promised joy,
    I from my mate retire:
        If she
        To me
    Preserve her vows divine
        And constant troth,
        She shall be both
    My love and Valentine.

SHEPHERD'S WEEK
JOHN GAY
(SELECTION FROM THURSDAY)
1685 – 1732

Last Valentine, the Day when Birds of Kind
Their Paramours with mutual Chirpings find;
I early rose, just at the break of Day,
Before the Sun had chased the Stars away;
A-field I went, amid the Morning Dew
To milk my Kine (for so should Housewives do)
Thee first I spied, and the first Swain we see,
In spite of Fortune shall our True-love be;
See, Lubberkin,[18] each Bird his Partner take,
And canst thou then thy Sweetheart dear forsake?
With my sharp Heel I three times mark the Ground,
And turn me thrice around, around, around.

---

[18] Lubberkin. A sort of fairy or brownie, hence the mysterious actions in the last two lines.

TO DORINDA, ON VALENTINE'S DAY
ANONYMOUS
1696

Look how, my dear, the feathered kind,
By mutual caresses joined,
Bill, and seem to teach us two
What we to love and custom owe.

Shall only you and I forbear
To meet, and make a happy pair?
Shall we alone delay to live?
This day an age of bliss may give.

But ah! When I the proffer make,
Still coyly you refuse to take
My heart I dedicate in vain,
The too mean present you disdain.

Yet, since the solemn time allows
To choose the object of our vows,
Boldly I dare profess my flame,
Proud to be yours by any name.

From a collection titled Satyrs of Boileau Imitated.

VALENTINE'S DAY DITTY
ANONYMOUS
LATE SEVENTEENTH CENTURY

Good morrow to you, Valentine;
Curl your locks as I do mine,
Two before and three behind
Good morrow to you, Valentine.

THE VALENTINE WREATH
JAMES MONTGOMERY
1771 – 1854

Rosy red the hills appear
With the light of morning,
Beauteous clouds, in ether clear,
All the east adorning;
White through the mist the meadows shine
Wake, my love, my Valentine!

For thy locks of raven hue,
Flowers of hoar-frost pearly,
Crocus-cups of gold and blue,
Snow-drops drooping early,
With Mezereon sprigs combine
Rise, my love, my Valentine!

O'er the margin of the flood,
Pluck the daisy peeping;
Through the covert of the wood,
Hunt the sorrel creeping;
With the little celandine
Crown my love, my Valentine.

Pansies, on their lowly stems
Scattered o'er the fallows;
Hazel-buds with crimson gems,
Green and glossy sallows;
Tufted moss and ivy-twine,
Deck my love, my Valentine.

Few and simple flow'rets these;
Yet, to me, less glorious
Garden-beds and orchard-trees!
Since this wreath victorious
Binds you now for ever mine,
O my Love, my Valentine.

WITH A GIFT ON SAINT VALENTINE'S DAY
THOMAS MOORE
1779 – 1852

They say thine eyes,
Like sunny skies,
    Thy chief attraction form;
I see no sunshine in thine eyes;
    They take me all by storm.

ON THE PARAGON OF EXCELLENCE
ANONYMOUS
AROUND 1780

All hail fair vestal, lovely gift of heaven,
Nourished in prudence and in wisdom given.
Neglect not this small present from a friend,
Esteem commences where fierce passions end.
Transcendent Fair resplendent star approve
His pleading reasons who thus seek your love,
Accept his proffers, take his heart in care.
Cherish his passion in a modest sphere.
How then will heaven our constancy commend.
Empyreal bounties happy moments send,
Refulgent blisses crown us to our end.

*This poem, found in a hand-written valentine, contains an
acrostic. The sequence of the first letters of each line form the
name Ann Thacher, presumably the person to which it was
written.*

A HYMN TO BISHOP SAINT VALENTINE
LEIGH HUNT
1784 – 1859

The day, the only day returns,
The true red letter day returns,
When summer time in winter burns;
When a February dawn
Is opened by two sleeves in lawn
Fairer than Aurora's fingers,
And a burst of all bird singers,
And a shower of billet-doux.[19]
Tingeing cheeks with rosy hues,
And over all a face divine.
Face good-natured, face most fine.
Face most anti-saturnine,
Even thine, yea, even thine.
Saint of sweethearts, Valentine!
See, he's dawning! See, he comes,
With the jewels on his thumbs
Glancing us a ruby ray
(For he's sun and all to-day)!
See his lily sleeves! and now
See the mitre[20] on his brow!
See his truly pastoral crook.
And beneath his arm his book
(Some sweet tome *De Arte Amandi*):[21]

---

[19] Billet-doux. Love letters.
[20] Mitre. The special hat that bishops wear.
[21] De Arte Amandi. On the Art of Love.

And his hair, 'twixt saint and dandy,
Lovelocks touching either cheek,
And black, though with a silver streak,
As though for age both young and old,
And his look, 'twixt meek and bold,
Bowing round on either side,
Sweetly lipped and earnest-eyed.
And lifting still, to bless the land,
His very gentlemanly hand.

Hail! oh hail! and thrice again
Hail, thou clerk of sweetest pen!
Connubialest of clergymen!
Exquisite bishop! — not at all
Like Bishop Bonner; no, nor Hall,
That gibing priest; nor Atterbury,
Although he was ingenious, very,
And wrote the verses on the "Fan;"
But then he swore, — unreverend man!
But very like good Bishop Berkeley,
Equally benign and clerkly;
Very like Rundle, Shipley, Hoadley,
And all the genial of the godly;
Like De Sales, and like De Paul;
But most, I really think, of all.
Like Bishop Mant, whose sweet theology
Includeth verse and ornithology,
And like a proper rubric star,
Hath given us a new "Calendar,"
So full of flowers and birdly talking,
'Tis like an Eden bower to walk in.

Such another See is thine,
O thou Bishop Valentine;
Such another, but as big
To that, as Eden to a fig;
For all the world's thy diocese,
All the towns and all the trees,
And all the barns and villages:
The whole rising generation
Is thy loving congregation:
Enviable's indeed thy station;
Tithes cause thee no reprobation,
Dean and chapter's no vexation,
Heresy's no spoliation.
Begged is thy participation;
No one wishes thee translation,
Except for some sweet explanation.
All decree thee consecration!
    Beatification!
    Canonization!
All cry out, with heart-prostration.
Sweet's thy text-elucidation,
Sweet, oh sweet's thy visitation,
And Paradise thy confirmation.

VALENTINE
THEODORE HOOK
1788 – 1841

Old Custom, which to-day allows
    Addresses such as this;
When timid lovers breather their vows, —
    And sing of promised bliss;
Emboldens one, who else would fear
    To make his feelings known,
To whisper in the fair one's ear
    A sorrow — all his own.

Old Custom says, that rhyming words
    Must form the Valentine;
Yet jingling verse but ill accords
    With sentiments like mine.
Beheld, like visions fair and bright,
    At once your power was proved,
No sooner seen, than lost to sight,
    No sooner known than loved.

The lightning's fire from angry skies
    An instant death can give,
And who shall meet those soul-fraught eyes,
    And yet unwounded live?
Unlike the wrathful flame of heaven,
    Their radiance they impart;
But not less sure the wound is given
    Which rankles in the heart.

The smile that decks that downy cheek
    To arch expression joined,
The goodness of the heart bespeak,
    And powers of the mind;
'T is seldom in the world we trace
    An union half so rare,
In one combining sense and grace,
    As talented as fair.

Again to meet — again to part —
    It may — it may not be;
The thought but grieves an aching heart
    For what am I to thee!
Then fare thee well, no breast can own
    A passion half so pure
As his who loves unseen, unknown,
    Nor ever hopes a cure.

VALENTINE TO A FAIR ARTIST
DAVID HARTLEY COLERIDGE
1796 – 1849

O, mistress of that lovely art
Which can to shadows form impart —
Can fix these evanescent tints,
Fainter by far than lovers' hints,
And bring the scenes we love to mind,
When we have left them far behind, —
Thou seest an image in thy glass
Which does e'en Raphael's art surpass,
But which Dan Cupid has been able
To copy in my heart's soft table.
How proud 'twould make a connoisseur
To have so beauteous a picture!
For me, I won, it ill contents me
To have a copy, but torments me,
Unless I might possess, as well,
That copy's fair original.

THE SURPRISE
HEINRICH HEINE
1797 – 1856

I dreamt I saw you yesternight,
    And clasped my hands about your eyes,
Nor dared to venture in your sight
    Until you pardoned the surprise.

So take my letter, Valentine,
    My name and mission quickly guess —
I fear to offer word or sign;
    I wait until you whisper "Yes."

AURELIA, A VALENTINE
THOMAS KIBBLE HERVEY
1799 – 1859

With gazing on those charms of thine
My soul grows sad and faint;
But, turning to Saint Valentine,
Who is a gentle saint,

Said I, the fair Aurelia keeps
Her spirit locked from me.
O, show my weary heart the hook
On which she hangs the key!

Her breast is like a frozen lake,
On whose cold brink I stand;
O, buckle on my spirit's skates,
And take me by the hand!

And lead thou, loving saint, the way
To where the ice is thin,
That it may break beneath my feet
And let a lover in.

I see the honey on her lip, —
Have pity, saint, on me,
And turn a lonely gentleman
Into a humble-bee.

Why is it that an eye whose light
Should feed but bright-hued petals.
In my poor heart makes only night,

And grows but stinging nettles?

Whatever men have sung of old
Of Cynthia or Aurelia,
Seems flat, and tame, and dull, and cold.
To paint the young Aurelia.

All voices in my dreams seem hers,
And, through my fancies looming.
All other forms put on the form
Of bright Aurelia's blooming.

Help, help, from thee, Saint Valentine!
Bring forth thy strongest spell,
Go boldly to her soul's shut gate.
And ring her spirit's bell.

That she may ope the door at last
Unto my long desire.
And I take up my chair for life
Beside her young heart's fire.

A WREATH OF VALENTINES
THOMAS KIBBLE HERVEY
1799 – 1859

I. The time draws nigh, on fragrant wing,
    Of summer beams and bells;
But Love comes faster than the spring,
    And works with sweeter spells.

To him, upon the unsunned breeze,
    Immortal odors float;
And they may sail o'er ice-bound seas.
    Who take his golden boat.

The primrose faints within thy hair,
    The snowdrop looketh pale;
There is not sunshine in the air.
    Nor singing on the gale.

Look in with those beloved eyes
    Upon this heart of mine;
Bloom, scent, and song will all arise.
    To hail my Valentine!

II. Soon to the Rose the Nightingale
    Shall breathe his tender lay;
But Love, that hath a sweeter tale,
    Must tell that tale to-day.
In sighs, which are the spirit's song.
    My soul is poured to thine;
And time grows young, and hope grows strong.
    To hail my Valentine.

Since darkened hearts Love maketh bright.
    What might he do for oars?
Make all their fancies speak in light,
    Their feelings grow in flowers.
Glad fancies, flinging song about,
    Like stars, the while they shine.
And feelings giving fragrance out
    Because they intertwine.

Wherever Love hath touched the ground.
    It is the time of roses;
Of fairy wreaths within whose round
    The sighing soul reposes.
O, take my spirit home to thine.
    Elsewhere 't is wintry weather.
Hearts only yield their bloom divine
    When two have bloomed together.

III. Now, blessed be Saint Valentine,
    By whose high leave I pour
Words in this gentle ear of thine
    I never dared before!
Each thing to-day, in glade or nook,
    May name its Valentine;
I read out boldly from Love's book,
    And, dearest, thou art mine!

The breeze hath found the wall-flower oat.
    And feedeth on its sigh.
The hunter bee now hunts about
    The violet's deep-blue eye:

Escaping from its icy chain.
        The river runneth free.
And so, my heart flings off its pain.
        And Cometh straight to thee!

A blessing on Saint Valentine!
        He is a good old saint,
And maketh strong to speak to thine
        My soul that was so faint.
And then he serves a spirit, sweet!
        More loving than his own:
His task, to lead Lore's pilgrim feet
        To Hymen's altar-throne.
So, blessings on Saint Valentine,
        I am his worshipper, and thine I

IV. Love on the Threshold
Love, lady, on his own bright mom.
        Hath brought me to thy door;
Thou wilt not let thy look be scorn.
        And Cupid on the floor.
To-day, for old Saint Valentine,
        He ringeth all his bells.
                And I am trusting, lady mine,
                To him and to his spells.

He sits to-day by every hearth.
        And sings to every heart, —
Li all the chorus of his mirth,
        Hath only thine no part?
O, coldness never looked before
        From loving eyes like thine;

73

So, bid me, dearest, pass the door.
And claim my Valentine!

V. Love By the Church
The leaf is not upon the tree,
    The song-bird in the grove,
Yet hear I, as I gaze on thee,
    The singing of the dove.
Spring scents I cannot miss or prise[22]
    While feeding on thy breath,
        Nor do I seek for bright blue skies
        Whilst thou art underneath.

What care I that the stream be dim.
    Whilst thou art by the stream?
There cometh to my heart a hymn.
    And to mine eyes a gleam.
From yon old church, whose many bells
    Fling up to heaven their mirth,
Tet seem to whisper, "Heaven's spells
    May here be cast for earth."
        May such be to thy soul and mine
        The message of Saint Valentine!

VI. Love at Home

[*In allusion to a practice familiar on Valentine's morning in the North. The lover surprises his mistress, and blindfolds her with his hands.*]

Guess, and guess truly, lady mine,

---

[22] Prise. Take or gather in.

Who is abroad as thy Valentine?
Whose are the fingers, and whose is the tow,
That press on thy forehead, that blesseth thee now?
Love for such lore hath no need of his eyes.
To the loving the lover is known by his sighs.
O for a spell on thy lips of love's art!
Say, is my name, dearest, writ on thy heart?

Surely thy soul and thy brow understand
The voice of my spirit, the clasp of my hand.
O, if they read not my riddle this morn,
That hand must be widowed, that spirit forlorn.
This is the day when in city and grove
Love is a wanderer seeking for love.
Who is the fond one now pleading for thine?
Guess, and guess truly, my own Valentine!

To the Fourteenth of February
Thomas Hood
1799 – 1845

No popular respect will I omit
To do the honor on this happy day,
When every loyal lover tasks his wit
His simple truth in studious rhymes to pay,
And to his mistress dear his hopes convey.
Rather thou knowest I would still outrun
All calendars with Love's, — whose date alway
Thy bright eyes govern better than the sun, —
For with thy favor was my life begun;
And still I reckon on from smiles to smiles,
And not by summers, for I thrive on none
But those thy cheerful countenance compiles:
O! if it be to choose and call thee mine,
Love, thou art every day my Valentine.

THE DOVE
WINTHROP MACKWORTH PRAED
1802 – 1839

Tell me, little darling Dove,
Whence and whither dost thou rove?

I am in haste; a brother tied
This doggerel greeting to my side;
May every good my sister bless,
Life, virtue, health, and happiness;
Not vulgar mirth, but modest sense;
Not mines of gold, but competence;
With these her bark may peaceful glide,
Uninjured, down life's swelling tide.
May soft Content's all-healing power
Stand ready for each suffering hour,
Enhance the good the Fates bestow,
And mitigate the pangs of woe.
Each year may an adoring crew
New Valentines around her strew;
Be every page, be every line,
As ardent, as sincere, as mine!

SONG FOR THE FOURTEENTH OF FEBRUARY
WINTHROP MACKWORTH PRAED
1802 – 1839

BY A GENERAL LOVER

"Mille gravem telis, eshausta pene pharetra"[23]

Apollo has peeped through the shutter
    And wakened the witty and fair
The boarding school belle's in a flutter
    The two penny-post in despair;
The breath of the morning is flinging
    A magic on blossom and spray;
And Cockneys and sparrows are singing,
    In chorus, on Valentine's day.

Away with ye, dreams of disaster;
    Away with ye, visions of law;
Of cases I never can master,
    Of pleadings I never shall draw,
Away with ye, parchments and papers;
    Red tapes, unread volumes, away;
It gives a fond lover the vapours
    To see you on Valentine's day!

I'll sit in my night-cap, like Hayley,
    I'll sit with my arms crossed like Spain,

---

[23] With a thousand weapons, his quiver almost being exhausted. From Ovid's *Metamorphoses*. Book 1, Line 443. From the story of Phoebus killing the Python, just before he sees Daphne.

Till joys, which are vanishing daily,
    Come back in their lustre again:
Oh! shall I look over the waters,
    Or shall I look over the way,
For the brightest and best of Earth's daughters,
    To rhyme to, on Valentine's Day?

Shall I crown with my worship, for fame's sake,
    Some goddess whom Fashion has starred,
Make puns on Miss Love and her namesake.
    Or pray for a *pas* with Brocard?
Then I flirt, in romantic idea.
    With Chester's adorable clay.
Or whisper in transport, "Si mea
    Cum Vestris"[24] — on Valentine's Day?

Shall I kneel to a Sylvia or Celia,
    Whom no one e'er saw, or may see,
A fancy-drawn Laura Amelia,
    An *ad libit*, Anna Marie?
Shall I court an initial with stars to it,
    Go mad for a G. or a J.,
Get Bishop to put a few bars to it,
    And print it on Valentine's Day?

I think not of Laura the witty;
    For, oh! she is married at York!
I sigh not for Rose of the City,

---

[24] If my prayers and yours had availed, [O Greeks, there would be no question as to the victor in this great strife, and you, Achilles, would still have your own armor, and we should still have you.] From Ovid's *Metamorphoses*, Book 13, line 128. From the story about the decision on the fate of Achilles' armor.

For, oh! she is buried at Cork;
Adèle has a braver and better
    To say — what I never could say;
Louise cannot construe a letter
    Of English, on Valentine's Day.

So perish the leaves in the arbour;
    The tree is all bare in the blast;
Like a wreck that is drifting to harbour,
    I come to thee, Lady, at last:
Where art thou, so lovely and lonely?
    Though idle the lute and the lay.
The lute and the lay are thine only,
    My fairest, on Valentine's Day.

For thee I have opened my Blackstone,
    For thee I have shut up myself;
Exchanged my long curls for a Caxton,
    And laid my short whist on the shelf;
For thee I have sold my old sherry.
    For thee I have burned my new play;
And I grow philosophical, — very!
    Except upon Valentine's Day!

WHEN I FIRST BEHELD THY FACE
ANONYMOUS
ABOUT 1807

O when I first beheld thy face
And pressed in mine thy gentle hand,
Thy blooming cheek and modest grace
Waved o'er my sole a magic wand;
Thy kindly tone, thy playful smile,
Bespeaking innocence and love,
The lustre of thine eyes the while
That beamed like angel orbs above, —
All joined upon my heart to pour
A joyance never felt before!

Life is a changeful scene, and we
May scarce have felt its sorrows yet,
But still, whate'er the prospects be,
The path howe'er with thorns beset,
Still true to thee and Heav'n above,
I'll seek no other valentine
For solace, but hold fast the love
That ever guides my soul to thine;
Still shall I to thy heart repair
And find my consolation there!

A VALENTINE ACROSTIC
EDGAR ALLAN POE
1809 – 1849

For her this rhyme is penned, whose luminous eyes,
Brightly expressive as the twins of Leda,
Shall find her own sweet name, that nestling lies
Upon the page, enwrapped from every reader.
Search narrowly the lines! - they hold a treasure
Divine - a talisman - an amulet
That must be worn at heart. Search well in the measure -
The words - the syllables! Do not forget
The trivialest point, or you may lose your labor
And yet there is in this no Gordian knot
Which one might not undo without a sabre,
If one could merely comprehend the plot.
Enwritten upon the leaf where now are peering
Eyes scintillating soul, there lie perdus
Three eloquent words oft uttered in the hearing
Of poets, by poets - as the name is a poet's, too,
Its letters, although naturally lying
Like the knight Pinto - Mendez Ferdinando -
Still form a synonym for Truth - Cease trying!
You will not read the riddle, though you do the best you
can do.

The acrostic reads "Frances Sargent Osgood." As Poe was a great admirer of her work, he published several poems of "Fanny" Osgood.

THE LAWYER'S VALENTINE
JOHN GODFREY SAXE
1816 – 1887

I'm notified, fair neighbor mine,
    By one of our profession,
That this— the Term of Valentine —
    Is Cupid's Special Session.

Permit me therefore to report
    Myself on this occasion,
Quite ready to proceed to Court,
    And File my Declaration.

I've an Attachment for you, too;
    A legal and a strong one;
O, yield unto the Process, do;
    Nor let it be a long one!

No scowling bailiff lurks behind;
    He'd be a precious noddy,[25]
Who, failing to Arrest the mind,
    Should go and take the Body!

For though a form like yours might throw
    A sculptor in distraction;
I couldn't serve a Capias — no —
    I'd scorn so base an Action!

O do not tell me of your youth,

---

[25] Noddy. Simpleton, fool.

And turn away demurely;
For though you're very young, in truth,
    You're not an Infant, surely!

The Case is everything to me;
    My heart is love's own tissue;
Don't plead a Dilatory Plea;
    Let's have the General Issue!

Or, — since you've really no defense,
    Why not, this present Session,
Omitting all absurd pretense,
    Give judgment by Confession?

So shall you be my loving wife
    And I — your faithful lover
Be Tenant of your heart for Life,
    With no Remainder over.

A VALENTINE
JAMES T. FIELDS
1817 – 1881

She that is fair, though never vain or proud,
More fond of home, than fashion's changing crowd;
Whose taste refined even female friends admire,
Dressed not for show, but robed in neat attire;
She who has learned, with mild, forgiving breast,
To pardon frailties, hidden or confessed;
True to herself, yet willing to submit,
More swayed by love than ruled by worldly wit;
Though young, discreet, — though ready, ne'er unkind,
Blessed with no pedant's, but a Woman's mind; —
She wins our hearts, toward her our thoughts incline,
So at her door go leave my Valentine.

Valentine's Day, 1873
Charles Kingsley
1819 – 1875

Oh! I wish I were a tiny browny bird from out the south,
Settled among the alder-holts, and twittering by the stream;
I would put my tiny tail down, and put up my tiny mouth,
And sing my tiny life away in one melodious dream.
I'd sing about the blossoms, and the sunshine and the sky.
And the tiny wife I meant to have in such a cosy nest;
And if someone came and shot me dead, then I could but die,
With my tiny life and tiny song just ended at their best.

SAINT VALENTINE'S DAY
THOMAS WILLIAM PARSONS
1819 – 1892

This day was sacred, once, to Pan,
And kept with song and wine;
But when our better creed began
'T was held no more divine,
Until there came a holy man,
One Bishop Valentine.

He, finding, as all good men will
Much in the ancient way
That was not altogether ill,
Restored the genial day;
And we the pagan fashion still
With pious hearts obey.

Without this custom, all would go
Amiss in Love's affairs,
All passion would be poor dumb show,
Pent sighs, and secret prayers;
And bashful maids would never know
What timid swain was theirs.

Ah! many things with mickle[26] pains
Without reward are done,
A thousand poets rack their brains
For her who loves but one;
Yea, many weary with their strains

---

[26] Mickle. Great, strong.

The nymph that cares for none.

Yet, should no faithful heart be faint
To give affection's sign:
So, dearest, let mine own acquaint
With its emotion — thine;
And blessings on that fine old Saint,
Good Bishop Valentine!

THE SWEETS OF LOVE, OR VALENTINE'S DAY
ANONYMOUS
1820

The morning was fair, and all nature round was gay
I met with young Flora, and thus to her did say,
Arise my sweet charmer, and make no delay,
And meet your true lover on Valentine's Day.

This blooming young damsel did quickly arise,
And said, "gentle swain you do me much surprise,
What think you my dad my mammy will say,
If I should go with you, though it is Valentine's Day.

As for your dad and mammy, you leave that to me,
Never fear but they and I we soon shall agree.
Hark! The birds how they sing, and the lambs sport & play,
To welcome the suites of Valentine's Day.

This fair maiden she willingly gave her consent,
So then arm in arm over the meadows they went,
Where they ganged[27] to the church, so loving and gay,
And they bless the sweet times of Valentine's Day.

So now in sweet wedlock the knot it is tied,
This young Swain he is blessed with a beautiful bride.
The lads and the lasses, so merry and gay,
Danced on the green on Valentine's Day

The Music so delightful and Charming did sound,
Made the groves and valleys to ring, such mirth did abound,
So I'd have you good harm humoured, ye blooming and gay,
No doubt you'll get wedded on Valentine's Day.

---

[27] Ganged. Went. (Going-ed.)

TO AN OLD-TIME VALENTINE
ANONYMOUS
ABOUT 1827

Tell me you love me; I know it full well,
    Though of truths so delightful one can't be too sure;
Doubts will arise that a breath may dispel,
    Fears that alone such avowals can cure.
When were those syllables murmured in vain?
Tell me you love me again and again.

Tell me you love me, though often before
    You have told me the tale I now bid you repeat;
Outpourings like these from the lips we adore
    In their food iteration grow daily more sweet;
Why from the tender confession refrain?
Tell me you love me again and again.

LOVE'S LOVERS
DANTE GABRIEL ROSSETTI
1828 – 1882

Some ladies love the jewels in Love's zone,
And gold-tipped darts he hath for painless play
In idle scornful hours he flings away;
And some that listen to his lute's soft tone
Do love to vaunt the silver praise their own;
Some prize his blindfold sight; and there be they
Who kissed his wings which brought him yesterday
And thank his wings to-day that he is flown.
My lady only loves the heart of Love:
Therefore Love's heart, my lady, hath for thee
His bower of unimagined flower and tree:
There kneels he now, and all-anhungered of
Thine eyes grey-lit in shadowing hair above,
Seals with thy mouth his immortality.

"LOVE HAS NO WINTER HOURS"
(SAINT VALENTINE'S DAY 1881)
CHRISTINA G. ROSSETTI
1830 – 1894

Too cold almost for hope of Spring
    Or first-fruits from the realm of flowers,
Your dauntless Valentine, I bring
    One sprig of love, and sing
    "Love has no Winter hours" —.
If even in this world love is love
    (This wintry world which felt the Fall),
What must it be in Heaven above
    Where love to great and small
        Is all in all?

LINES SUGGESTED BY THE FOURTEENTH OF FEBRUARY
(VERSION 1)
CHARLES STUART CALVERLEY
1831 – 1884

Ere the morn the East has crimsoned,
    When the stars are twinkling there,
(As they did in Watts's Hymns, and
    Made him wonder what they were
When the forest-nymphs are beading
    Fern and flower with silvery dew —
My infallible proceeding
    Is to wake, and think of you.

When the hunter's ringing bugle
    Sounds farewell to field and copse,
And I sit before my frugal
    Meal of gravy-soup and chops:
When (as Gray remarks) "the moping
    Owl doth to the moon complain,"
And the hour suggests eloping -
    Fly my thoughts to you again.

May my dreams be granted never?
    Must I aye endure affliction
Rarely realised, if ever,
    In our wildest works of fiction?
Madly Romeo loved his Juliet;
    Copperfield began to pine
When he hadn't been to school yet -
    But their loves were cold to mine.

Give me hope, the least, the dimmest,
    Ere I drain the poisoned cup:
Tell me I may tell the chemist
    Not to make that arsenic up!
Else, this heart shall soon cease throbbing;
    And when, musing o'er my bones,
Travelers ask, "Who killed Cock Robin?"
    They'll be told, "Miss Sarah J-s."

LINES SUGGESTED BY THE FOURTEENTH OF FEBRUARY (VERSION 2)
CHARLES STUART CALVERLEY
1831 – 1884

Darkness succeeds to twilight:
Through lattice and through skylight
The stars no doubt, if one looked out,
    Might be observed to shine:
        And sitting by the embers
        I elevate my members
        On a stray chair, and then and there
    Commence a Valentine.

Yea! by Saint Valentinus,
Emma shall not be minus
What all young ladies, whate'er their grade is,
    Expect to-day no doubt:
        Emma the fair, the stately -
        Whom I beheld so lately,
        Smiling beneath the snow-white wreath
    Which told that she was "out."

Wherefore fly to her, swallow,
And mention that I'd "follow,"
And "pipe and trill," et cetera, till
    I died, had I but wings:
        Say the North's "true and tender,"
        The South an old offender;
        And hint in fact, with your well-known tact,
    All kinds of pretty things.

Say I grow hourly thinner,
Simply abhor my dinner —
Though I do try and absorb some viand
    Each day, for form's sake merely:
        And ask her, when all's ended,
        And I am found extended,
        With vest blood-spotted and cut carotid,
    To think on Her's sincerely.

TO A LADY
ANONYMOUS
1833

Add you forever faithless fair
You are not a worth of thought or care
    Ever up on Pleasures wing
    All foolish flaunting fickle thing
All bubble guilt, a painted toy
Domestic Comfort to destroy
    Cured be his fate who chooses thee!
    He'd better cling to Tyburn's tree,[28]
And dance a full hour in the air,
Than a marriage life with you to share.
    Thank heaven from your chains I'm free.
    You are no Valentine for me!

---

[28] Tyburn's tree. The name for the gallows in the town of Tyburn in Middlesex, England (also known as the King's Gallows), where between 1196 and 1783 thousands of people lost their lives.

VALENTINE
JOHN JAMES PIATT
1835 - 1917

To her whose heart has made her lovely face
A Heaven for its sweet roses; her whose grace
Of thought and word and deed forever seems
The light of some sweet angel in her soul,
Stealing from Heaven in still, half conscious dreams:
Go, little Doves, and bear this gentle scroll
(Bearing my heart) to her — ah, if she smiles,
You need not tell: I'd know it a thousand miles!
Go, little Doves, to her for whom I pine
And softly whisper: "Here's your Valentine."

TO A LADY WITH A RING
H. CHOLOMONDELEY-PERNELL
1837 – 1915

Sweet Valentine, dear Lady Mine,
Love lays an offering at your shrine;
Yet seeks not by this span of gold
That which would reach through year untold,
Would burn when life itself is cold.
Not with the dazzling fitful gleam
That gilds the stripling's fever-dream
(For love, the dream-love of the boy,
Is but a glimmering summer toy).
But with the strong and steady glow,

But with the deep and tender flow,
That a man's heart alone can know,
Pouring his soul out at her feet
Whose smile can make all dark things sweet.
Love undivided, close and dear,
With ready arm to guide and cheer,
His breast her shield from every fear, —
Love, changeless still, where change is rife,
Through storm and calm, through peace and strife,
For grief, for joy, for death, for life!
Love breathed in one soft whisper — Wife.

DAISY'S VALENTINES
AUSTIN DOBSON
1840 – 1921

All night through Daisy's sleep, it seems,
    Have ceaseless "rat-taps" thundered;
All night through Daisy's rosy dreams
    Have devious Postmen blundered,
Delivering letters round her bed, —
Suggestive missives, sealed with red,
And franked of course with due Queen's head, —
    While Daisy lay and wondered.

But now, when chirping birds begin,
    And Day puts off the Quaker, —
When Cook renews her morning din
    And rates the cheerful baker, —
She dreams her dream no dream at all,
For, just as pigeons come at call,
Winged letters flutter down and fall
    Around her head, and wake her.

Yes, there they are! With quirk and twist
    And fraudful art directed;
(Save Grandpapa's dear still old "fist,"
    Through all disguise detected;)
But which is his, — her young Lothair's,[29] —
Who wooed her on the school-room stairs
With three sweet cakes, and two ripe pears

---

[29] Lothair. Usually an irresponsible lover, but here used lightly to mean
a young sweetheart.

100

In one neat pile collected?

'Tis there, be sure. Though truth to speak,
    (If truth may be permitted),
I doubt that young "gift-bearing Greek"
    Is scarce for fealty fitted;
For has he not (I grieve to say),
To two loves more on this same day,
In just the same emblazoned way,
    His transient vows transmitted?

He *may* be true. Yet, Daisy dear,
    That even youth grown colder
You'll find is no new thing, I fear;
    And when you're somewhat older,
You'll read of one Dardanian boy
Who "wooed with gifts" a maiden coy, —
Then took the morning train to Troy
    In spite of all he'd told her.

But wait. Your time will come, and then
    Obliging Fates, please send her
The bravest thing you have in men,
    Sound-hearted, strong, and tender; —
The kind of man, dear Fates, you know,
That feels how shyly Daisies grow,
And what soft things they are, and so
    Will spare to spoil or mend her.

WHEN I THINK OF THEE
ANONYMOUS
ABOUT 1840

I think of thee in the night,
    When all beside is still
And the moon comes out, with her pale, sad light
    To sit on the lonely hill!
When the stars are all like dreams,
    And the breezes all like sighs,
And there comes a voice from the far-off streams,
    Like thy spirit's low replies!

I think of thee by day,
    'Mid the cold and busy crowd,
When the laughter of the young and gay
    Is far too glad and loud!
I hear thy soft, sad tone,
    And thy young, sweet smile I see —
My heart — my heart were all alone,
    But for its dreams of thee!

SAINT VALENTINE'S DAY
WILFRED SCAWEN BLUNT
1840 – 1942

To-day, all day, I rode upon the down,
With hounds and horsemen, a brave company
On this side in its glory lay the sea,
On that the Sussex weald, a sea of brown.
The wind was light, and brightly the sun shone,
And still we galloped on from gorse to gorse:
And once, when checked, a thrush sang, and my horse
Pricked his quick ears as to a sound unknown.
I knew the Spring was come. I knew it even
Better than all by this, that through my chase
In bush and stone and hill and sea and heaven
I seemed to see and follow still your face.
Your face my quarry was. For it I rode,
My horse a thing of wings, myself a god.

A BALLAD
B. MONTGOMERIE RANKIN
1841 – 1888

When summer leaves were green and wide,
    And sultry was the weather,
Home went two lovers side by side,
    From raking hay together;
        And he might plead and sue his fill,
        But she said naught — yet listened still.

And when the woods were bleak and bare,
    And skies were gray and freezing,
Still came no answer to his prayer,
    Nor to his trouble easing;
        And he must mourn his heavy fate,
        Who sought in vain his fancied mate.

Come, own my love and constant truth!
    You not so sore have tried me,
Yet let the crowning of our youth
    No longer be denied me;
        So coming spring shall garlands twine
        To deck my dainty Valentine.

MY GOLD AND ROSE VALENTINE
ANONYMOUS
ABOUT 1843

Gold gleams in the sunset sky behind you;
    Gold clasps the curve of your arms so fair;
Gold encircles your throat so perfect,
    And rippling gold is your hair.

Roses drop in the dusk above you;
    Roses faint at your fingertips;
Roses glow ardent red around you,
    And roses ardent red are your lips.

Valentine in the Form of a Ballad
Andrew Lang
1844 – 1912

The soft wind from the south land sped,
 He set his strength to blow,
From forests where Adonis bled,
 And lily flowers a-row:
 He crossed the straits like streams that flow,
The ocean dark as wine,
 To my true love to whisper low,
To be your Valentine.

The Spring half-raised her drowsy head,
 Besprent with drifted snow,
"I'll send an April day," she said,
 "To lands of wintry woe."
 He came,—the winter's overthrow
With showers that sing and shine,
 Pied daisies round your path to strow,
To be your Valentine.

Where sands of Egypt, swart and red,
 'Neath suns Egyptian glow,
In places of the princely dead,
 By the Nile's overflow,
 The swallow preened her wings to go,
And for the North did pine,
 And fain would brave the frost her foe,
To be your Valentine.

ENVOY

Spring, Swallow, South Wind, even so,
    Their various voice combine;
But that they crave on *me* bestow,
    To be your Valentine.

TO MY DAUGHTER
WALTER LEARNED
1847 – 1914

Her kiss is warm upon my cheek,
 She is not coy nor shy;
Her arms were clinging round my neck
 When she bade me good-bye.

She whispers soft her love for me,
 And I tell her of mine;
Sweetheart, no other maid could be
 So dear a Valentine.

She loves me more than all the world;
 Yet sadly I foresee,
As time rolls on, some other swain
 May be preferred to me.

Were she sixteen, instead of three,
 This little Daughter mine,
Another's vows might prove more dear
 Than Papa's Valentine.

VALENTINE
JAMES JEFFREY ROCHE
1847 – 1908

Great Antony, I drink to thee,
    The Roman lover bold,
Who knew the worth of love and earth
    And gave the dross for gold.

Rich Antony, I envy thee,
    Who hadst a world to stake,
And, win or lose, didst bravely choose
    To risk it for Her sake.

Poor Antony, I pity thee,
    So small a world was thine
I'd scorn to lay the prize to-day
    Before my Valentine!

To My Valentine
Anonymous
About 1850

Thou art lovelier than the coming
    Of fairest flowers of spring,
When the wild bee wanders humming,
    Like a bless'd fairy thing:
Thou art lovelier than the breaking
    Of orient crimsoned morn,
When the gentlest winds are shaking
    The dewdrops from the thorn.

I have seen the wild flowers springing,
    In wood, and field, and glen,
Where a thousand birds were singing,
    And my thoughts were of thee then;
For there's nothing gladsome round me,
    Or beautiful to see,
Since thy beauty's spell has bound me,
    But is eloquent of thee.

A VALENTINE
EUGENE FIELD
1850 – 1895

O Princess, what shall I bring
To offer before thy throne?
For I know of no joyous thing
That is not already thine own.
Youth and beauty and love
Desirest thou more than these?
Lo, from the skies above
And from far away mystical seas,
All things radiant and rare
All things tender and sweet,
Hasten, O Princess fair,
To fall in delight at thy feet.
So, Princess, what shall I bring,
When low I bend at thy throne?
"My heart for an offering,"
E'en that has been long thine own.

THE VALENTINE
EUGENE FIELD
1850 – 1895

My Valentine's a page of gold,
Upon it by the morning light
I trace new hopes and fancies bright,
So sweetly is the story told,
That old, old story, yet so new,
A little song of love, a voice
That bids my faltering soul rejoice,
A promise to be ever true;
O love, sweet love, this honest heart
Unknown to coquetry or art,
Hath sworn fidelity to you.
And to my trustful heart I press
My valentine, with fond caress.
But still as sweetly as of old,
And now the long, long years have fled,
1 read the treasured sheet of gold.
What though my love, alas! be dead
And as I read from yonder skies
An angel with a radiant crown
Comes to my lovely chamber down
And bids me dry my streaming eyes.
So in the soft declining day
I think of him who's far away,
Whose body in the churchyard lies.
And to my broken heart I press
My valentine, with fond caress.

MAMMA'S VALENTINE
EUGENE FIELD
1850 – 1895

Baby came toddling up to my knee,
    His chubby features all aglow,
    "Dess I'se doin' to be 'oor beau,
See what oo' dot from me!"[30]
A valentine from my baby boy!
    A crumpled sheet and a homely scrawl,
    In a baby hand — that was all —
Yet it filled my heart with joy.

Broken my heart and white my hair,
    And my mother's eyes are used to weep;
    My little boy is fast asleep
In the churchyard over there.
What shall be mamma's valentine? —
    The spirit touch of the baby hand,
    A baby voice from the spirit land
Singing a song divine.

---

[30] "Guess I'm going to be your beau. See what you got from me!"

A VALENTINE TO MY WIFE
EUGENE FIELD
1850 – 1895

Accept, dear girl, this little token,
And if between the lines you seek,
You'll find the love I've often spoken—
The love my dying lips shall speak.

Our little ones are making merry
O'er am'rous ditties rhymed in jest,
But in these words (though awkward—very)
The genuine article's expressed.

You are as fair and sweet and tender,
Dear brown-eyed little sweetheart mine,
As when, a callow youth and slender,
I asked to be your Valentine.

What though these years of ours be fleeting?
What though the years of youth be flown?
I'll mock old Tempus with repeating,
"I love my love and her alone!"

And when I fall before his reaping,
And when my stuttering speech is dumb,
Think not my love is dead or sleeping,
But that it waits for you to come.

So take, dear love, this little token,
And if there speaks in any line
The sentiment I'd fain have spoken,
Say, will you kiss your Valentine?

SAINT VALENTINE
ANONYMOUS
1851

I think if Saint Valentine but knew
the way his fete day now's commemorated
And if the strange productions met his view
That fill our picture-shops, at any rate he's
Be much amused, and, no doubt, marvel too,
At fame he surely scarce anticipated—
A fame as great as any of the ages
Of Greece, or Rome, or of the Middle Ages.

T wonder what his saintship had to do
With flaming hearts, or with the cooing dove,
With little bows and arrows, and the true
Entangled lover's knot (fit type of love);
With chubby, flying Cupisds, peeping through
The leaves of roses, or through clouds above,
Daintily sketched on paper, with lace edges,
To be perhaps of timid love the pledges.

The Sacred Nine, by many youthful poet,
Are now invoked, and many a wasted quire
Of cream-laid note-paper will serve to show it,
Covered with scraps of wild poetic fire,
And bursts of eloquence! No doubt you know it,
By observation, or experience dire.
What crooked stanzas will be perpetrated
By bards and rhymesters uninitiated!

They'll scarce improve upon the doggerel verse,
That tells of "roses red and violets blue;"
And ends by saying, in a style most terse,
That the "carnation's sweet, and so are you."
I have seen modern rhymes that are much worse,
But then I have seen better, it is true;
Exquisite songs and sonnets bright and pure,
The gems of minstrelsy and literature.

How many eyes are sparkling with love-light,
As loving words are read; and what commotion
When postmen knock! What ill-conceived delight,
When these mysterious tokens of devotion,
Tinted and scented, meet the dear one's sight!
But I'm on dangerous ground and rather blundering,
So I'll return to where I left off wondering.

Wondering about Saint Valentine's connection
With this sort of thing so unmonastic,
Suggesting something like a dereliction
From the prescribed high roads ecclesiastic,
'Twould seem his heart was in the wrong direction,
And for an ancient bishop far too plastic;
He's certainly the Cupid of Theology,
Rivalling the rosy boy of Old Mythology.

Perhaps he had a taste for wedding-cake,
Or orange blossoms in a white chip bonnet;
Perhaps the marriage fees he likes to take;
At least he never did (depend on it)
Treat marriage like Saint Paul, who seemed to make
A point of throwing ice-cold water on it.

I wonder whether, too, he wrote epistles,
Or spent his time illuminating missals?

If he did write at all, it was a lecture
On love I think, or something of the kind;
And much less calculated to correct your
Follies and foibles, than distract your mind;
But this is only founded on conjecture,
For not a line of his can I yet find,
Though I have searched through many darksome pages
Of the Church History of the Middle Ages.

And there I read, that in the eternal city,
Now nearly one thousand six hundred years ago,
Was doomed to death by Claudius Caesar—so
Our saint was martyred! —what dreadful pity!
What it was for, I don't exactly know,
(*He* didn't know perhaps); indeed his history
Remains to me a most intricate mystery.

Love live thy mem'ry, great Saint Valentine!
Still lend thy ancient name to lovers' lays,
And with thy spirit animate each line,
And still may poets celebrate thy praise,
And yearly help to make that name of thine
"Familiar in our mouths," as Shakespeare says,
"As Household Words."

— (This wish is loyal too,
        For Valentines increase with revenue.)

VALENTINE VERSES
FRANCIS WILLIAM BOURDILLON
1852 – 1921

I send a sign of love; the shower sends
    The breeze before it, whispering, "He is coming!"
And the glad field her leaves and flowers bends,
    And hushes all her myriad insects' humming.

I send a sign of love; the morning sends
    A rosy cloud, his mounted messenger;
And the glad earth in ecstasy attends,
    Sure now her love himself will come to her.

O fairer than the field, than the whole earth,
    Would that they lover's coming in thy sight
Were as the rain-cloud to a land of dearth,
    Were as the morning to a world of night!

A CLEAR-EYED CUPID
WILLIAM LINDSAY
1858 – 1922

Young Love, a playing in faire Celia's hair,
Became entangled in a golden snare,
And tearful vowed if she would set him free
He'd pay the ransom, whatso'er it be.

She loosed his light wings from the twisted tress,
And off he fluttered, free but weaponless;
For Celia took his quiver and swift bow
For ransom, ere she let the rascal go.

More merciless than Cupid, Celia is,
Clear-eyed, she shoots with surer aim than his;
And, if the quiver fail not, as we pray,
No man shall live, but bears a wound away.

AWAKE, AWAKE
(A RONDEL)
FRANK DEMPSTER SHERMAN
1860 – 1916

Awake, awake, O gracious heart,
There's someone knocking at the door;

The chilling breezes make him smart;
His little feet are tired and sore.
Arise, and welcome him before
Adown his cheeks the big tears start:

Awake, awake, O gracious heart,
There's someone knocking at the door.

'T is Cupid come with loving art
To honour, worship, and implore:
And lest, unwelcomed, he depart
With all his wise mysterious lore,

Awake, awake, O gracious heart,
There's someone knocking at the door.

MY VALENTINE
LAURENS MAYNARD
1866 – 1917

My little Valentine is fair.
 Her name — ah, don't you wish you knew?
All curling falls her soft brown hair
 And her dark eyes flash as the dew
On roses sparkles when the sun
Kisses the flowers it has won
 To open by its rays.

What shall I send my Valentine
 Upon this joyous festal day
While Cupid's arrows flash and shine
 Piercing my heart, though not to slay?
My wounded heart to her I'll send
That she, perchance, her love may lend
 To bring me happy days.

SPRING SMILES
ENIS HERNE
FLOURISHED IN THE 1870S

Spring smiles anew with myriad hue,
    And laughs aloud in the breeze;
Pours forth her song blithe nests among,
    Her dance in the waving trees:
And sweet such joys to hear and see,
Did but my Valentine rove with me!

Each path through life with flowers is rife,
    And mirth is born in the breast,
And every day has its song and play,
    And every age its zest:
And such long joys in store might be,
Would but my Valentine pair with me!

FEBRUARY
MARY BARKER DODGE
FLOURISHED IN THE 1880S

Wan, wind-wracked month, of all the months most bare
    Of outward beauty or of inward grace;
    Reserved of ancient custom to efface
By sacrificial offering, whate'er
Of taint was held to be the whole year's share:
    One day, at least, thy cold, gray arms embrace,
    That serves to set a dimple in thy face
And by its fairness make the rest more fair:
The happy day when birds begin to woo,
    And win fond mates, to bless the tiny nest,
    Already modelled in the tinier breast;
The happy day in which, sweet heart, for you,
    A rosier tint o'erspreads this breast of mine,
    Sending its message through Saint Valentine.

A SMOKER'S VALENTINE
(SHORTER VERSION)
LYRA NICOTIANA
NINETEENTH CENTURY

What's my love's name? Guess her name.
She reciprocates my flame,
Cheers me wheresoe'er I go;
Never forward, never coy,
She is evermore my joy.
Who could help but love her so?
Nicotina, mistress mine,
Thou shalt be my Valentine.

A SMOKER'S VALENTINE
(LONGER VERSION)
LYRA NICOTIANA
NINETEENTH CENTURY

What's my love's name? Guess her name.
Nina? No.
Alina? No.
It does end with "ina," though.
Guess again. Christina? No;
Guess again. Wilhelmina? No.
She reciprocates my flame,
Cheers me wheresoe'er I go;
Never forward, never coy,
She is evermore my joy.
Oh, the rapture! oh, the bliss!
When I met my darling's kiss.
Oh, I love her form to greet!
Oh, her breath is passing sweet!
Who could help but love her so?
Nicotina, mistress mine,
Thou shalt be my Valentine.

A VALENTINE
JEANNETTE BLISS GILLESPY
FLOURISHED IN THE EARLY 1900S

The wise forget, dear heart;
    They leave the past
And play the hero's part
    Brave to the last.

They weep not nor regret,
    Calm are their eyes.
Dear heart, the wise forget.
    I am not wise.

AN UNSENTIMENTAL VALENTINE
ELIZABETH P. ALLEN
FLOURISHED IN THE EARLY 1900S

If I met you face to face
Maiden fair and full of grace,
I should bow and doff my hat,
Say "your servant," and all that.

While I watched your pretty ways,
I could only smile and praise,
And you'd never dream your lover
Could a flaw in you discover.

But I'm bolder, Lady mine,
Hid behind Saint Valentine;
And I'll count you one, two, three
Faults that I can plainly see.

Once I saw a tempest rise,
Clouding o'er your pretty eyes,
When a guest came to the door\
Who was old and sad and poor.

Once I saw you turn away
With a cold and fretful "nay,"
When your little brother came
Begging for some childish game.

Once I saw you sit at ease
With a book upon your knees,
While your mother, patient saint,

Did your work without complaint.

Ah, my pretty Valentine,
Ere I ask you to be mine,
I must know that lovely face
Shines with more than surface grace,

That your captivating art
Does not hide a careless heart,
Lest when tresses brown grow white
Eyes get dim which now are bright,

Age and trouble come apace,
Stealing beauty from your face,
I should bitterly repine
Choosing you my Valentine.

THE REEDS
M. E. G.
FLOURISHED IN THE EARLY 1900S

To the reeds I will tell
That I love my love well
They shall whisper to her,
As their slender leaves stir,
That no other than she
Can my Valentine be.
To the brookside, oh, hie thee,[31]
Where halcyons hover,
And hark, while they sigh thee
A vow from thy lover.

---

[31] Hie thee. Hurry (you).

A VALENTINE
ANONYMOUS (FROM THE GERMAN)
AROUND 1900

I love thee!
Thou lov'st me!
That thou knowest
Verily!
Fast locked thou art
Within my heart —
And I have lost
The little key!

WITH A RING
BEARING A HEART AND THE MOTTO, "STOP, THIEF!"
ANONYMOUS
AROUND 1900

Soon as I saw your beautiful eyes,
    You played a roguish part;
You first enthralled me by surprise,
    Then robbed me of my heart!

CREDITS

The following poems or passages are original translations and thus fully copyrighted by The Primavera Press and Gerard P. NeCastro, 2017. All Rights Reserved.

Lady, Since You Do Not Care – Bertran de Born
A Lady Asks Me – Guido Cavalcanti
Where the Heart Is – John Gower
Whosoever Remains Alone – John Gower
Parliament of Fowls – Geoffrey Chaucer
Legend of Good Women – Geoffrey Chaucer
Complaint of Mars – Geoffrey Chaucer
Complaint of Love – Geoffrey Chaucer
The Book of Cupid – John Clanvowe
Saint Valentine's Dream – Otton de Granson
Good Thomas the Friar – Anonymous
Song of the Rose – Christine de Pisan
A String of Beads – Christine de Pisan
To my Sovereign Lady – John Lydgate
To Her That Excels them All – John Lydgate
Charter of the Court of Love – Alain Chartier
Farewell to Love – Charles of Orleans
For His Valentine – William Fowler

The remainder of the works in this edition are in the public domain, though most have been modernized. Before quoting any of these poems, be sure to check the original edition.

SPECIAL THANKS

To Debra Kirouac, one of our finest emerging writers, for her suggestion on the title for this volume.

To Frank Salvia, one of the finest uncles in the world, for his suggestion on the name of the preface.

To Vicki, my wife, the finest of all Valentines, for her patience and advice.

www.ingramcontent.com/pod-product-compliance
Lightning Source LLC
Chambersburg PA
CBHW022008100426
42736CB00041B/1154